Laws
of
Association
Football
Guide for
Players
and Referees
1996–1997

Authorized by the International Football
Association Board

Revised edition from 1 July 1996

PAN BOOKS

This edition published 1996 by Pan Books
an imprint of Macmillan Publishers Ltd
25 Eccleston Place, London, SW1W 9NF
and Basingstoke

Associated companies throughout the world

ISBN 0 330 34767 5

9 8 7 6 5 4 3 2 1

A CIP catalogue record for this book is available from the British Library

Phototypeset by Intype London
Printed and bound in Great Britain by Mackays of Chatham PLC

Contents

Amendments to Laws and International Board Decisions made in 1996 are indicated by side lines.
Each Law should be read in conjunction with the appropriate International Board Decision.

Introduction

The International FA Board, comprising representatives of the four British Associations and the FIFA, meets annually and its decisions are binding on all National Associations. No alterations to the Laws of the Game may be made by any Association until they have been passed by the Board.

The International Board is of the opinion that the Laws should be kept as simple and straightforward as possible and that differences of application should be resolved by 'rulings or decisions', rather than by further definitions of Law.

The Council of The Football Association have decided that, in England, instructions regarding the Laws of the Game will be issued only by The Football Association.

Laws of Association Football – Guide for Players and Referees (formerly the *Referees' Chart*) is an official FA publication and is designed to be of benefit to participants and supporters of the game of football.

Notes

Subject to the agreement of the National Association concerned and provided the principles of these Laws are maintained, the Laws may be modified in their application to matches for players of under 16 years of age, for Women's football and for Veterans' football (over 35 years).

Any or all of the following modifications are permissible:–
    (a) dimensions of the field of play;
    (b) size, weight and material of the ball;
    (c) width between the goal-posts and height of the cross-bar from the ground;
    (d) the duration of the periods of play;
    (e) number of substitutions.

Further modifications are only possible with the consent of the International Football Association Board.

References to the male gender within the Laws of the Game in respect of Referees, Assistant Referees, Players or Officials are for simplification and refer to both males and females.

The Field of Play

(1) **Dimensions** The field of play shall be rectangular, its length being not more than 130 yards nor less than 100 yards and its breadth not more than 100 yards nor less than 50 yards. (In International Matches the length shall be not more than 120 yards nor less than 110 yards and the breadth not more than 80 yards nor less than 70 yards.) The length shall in all cases exceed the breadth.

(2) **Marking** The field of play shall be marked with distinctive lines, not more than 5 inches in width, not by a V-shaped rut, in accordance with the plan, the longer boundary lines being called the touch-lines and the shorter the goal-lines. A flag on a post not less than 5 feet high and having a non-pointed top, shall be placed at each corner; a similar flag-post may be placed opposite the halfway-line on each side of the field of play, not less than 1 yard outside the touch-line. A halfway-line shall be marked out across the field of play. The centre of the field of play shall be indicated by a suitable mark and a circle with a 10 yards radius shall be marked round it.

(3) **The Goal-Area** At each end of the field of play two lines shall be drawn at right-angles to the goal-line, 6 yards from each goal-post. These shall extend into the field of play for a distance of 6 yards and shall be joined by a line drawn parallel with the goal-line. Each of the spaces enclosed by these lines and the goal-line shall be called the goal-area.

(4) **The Penalty-Area** At each end of the field of play two lines shall be drawn at right-angles to the goal-line, 18 yards from each goal-post. These shall extend into the field of play for a distance of 18 yards and shall be joined by a line drawn parallel with the goal-line. Each of the spaces enclosed by these lines and the goal-line shall be called a penalty-area. A suitable mark shall be made

The Field of Play and appurtenances shall be as shown in the plan below.

within each penalty-area, 12 yards from the mid-point of the goal-line, measured along an undrawn line at right angles thereto. These shall be the penalty-kick marks. From each penalty-kick mark an arc of a circle, having a radius of 10 yards, shall be drawn outside the penalty-area.

(5) **The Corner-Area** From each corner flag-post a quarter circle, having a radius of 1 yard, shall be drawn inside the field of play.

(6) **The Goals** The goals shall be placed on the centre of each goal-line and shall consist of two upright posts, equidistant from the corner-flags and 8 yards apart (inside measurement), joined by a horizontal cross-bar the lower edge of which shall be 8 ft. from the ground. For safety reasons, the goals, including those which are portable, must be anchored securely to the ground. The width and depth of the cross-bars shall not exceed 5 inches (12 cm). The goal-posts and the cross-bars shall have the same width.

Nets may be attached to the posts, cross-bars and ground behind the goals. They should be appropriately supported and be so placed as to allow the goalkeeper ample room.

INTERNATIONAL BOARD DECISIONS

1 In International Matches the dimensions of the field of play shall be: maximum 110 metres × 75 metres; minimum 100 metres × 64 metres.

2 National Associations must adhere strictly to these dimensions. Each National Association organizing an International Match must advise the Visiting Association, before the match, of the place and the dimensions of the field of play.

3 The Board has approved this table of measurements for the Laws of the Game.

	Metres			*Metres*
130 yards ..	.. 120	1 yard ..	..	1
120 yards ..	.. 110	8 feet ..	..	2.44
110 yards ..	.. 100	5 feet ..	..	1.50
100 yards ..	.. 90	28 inches..	..	0.71
80 yards ..	.. 75	27 inches..	..	0.68
70 yards ..	.. 64	9 inches..	..	0.22
50 yards ..	.. 45	5 inches..	..	0.12
18 yards ..	.. 16.50	$\frac{1}{2}$ inch ..	..	12.7 mm
12 yards ..	.. 11	$\frac{3}{8}$ inch ..	..	10 mm
10 yards ..	.. 9.15	14 oz. = 396 grams		
8 yards ..	.. 7.32	16 oz. = 453 grams		
6 yards ..	.. 5.50	8.5 lb./sq.in. = 600 gr/cm²		
		15.6 lb./sq. in. = 1,100 gr/cm²		

4 The goal-line shall be marked the same width as the depth of the goal-posts and the cross-bar so that the goal-line and goal-posts will conform in the same interior and exterior edges.

5 The 6 yards (for the outline of the goal-area) and the 18 yards (for the outline of the penalty-area) which have to be measured along the goal-line, must start from the inner sides of the goal-posts.

6 The space within the inside areas of the field of play includes the width of the lines marking these areas.

7 All Associations shall provide standard equipment, particularly in International Matches, when the Laws of the Game must be complied with in every respect and especially with regard to the size of the ball and other equipment which must conform to the regulations. All cases of failure to provide standard equipment must be reported to the FIFA.

8 In a match played under the rules of a competition if the cross-bar becomes displaced or broken play shall be stopped and the match abandoned unless the cross-bar has been repaired and replaced in position or a new one provided without such being a danger to the players. A rope is not considered to be a satisfactory substitute for a cross-bar.

In a friendly match, by mutual consent, play may be resumed without the cross-bar provided it has been removed and no longer constitutes a danger to the players. In these circumstances, a rope may be used as a substitute for a cross-bar. If a rope is not used and the ball crosses the goal-line at a point which in the opinion of the Referee is below where the cross-bar should have been he shall award a goal.

The game shall be restarted by the Referee dropping the ball at the place where it was when play was stopped, unless it was within the goal area at that time, in which case it shall be dropped on that part of the goal-area line which runs parallel to the goal-line, at the point nearest to where the ball was when play was stopped.

9 National Associations may specify such maximum and minimum dimensions for the cross-bars and goal-posts, within the limits laid down in **Law I**, as they consider appropriate.

10 Goal-posts and cross-bars must be made of wood, metal or other approved material as decided from time to time by the International FA Board. They may be square, rectangular, round, half round, or elliptical in shape. Goal-posts and cross-bars made of other materials and in other shapes are not permitted. The goal-posts must be of white colour.

11 Any kind of publicity is forbidden in connection with, or on, the field of play. In particular, no advertising material may be displayed at any level on nets, corner flags or goalposts, nor shall such appurtenances of the game have any extraneous equipment attached to them (cameras, microphones, etc.). The reproduction

7

of a FIFA, Confederation, National Association, League, Club or any other logo on the field of play (turf) is also forbidden.

12 'Curtain-raisers' to International Matches should only be played following agreement on the day of the match, and taking into account the condition of the field of play, between representatives of the two Associations and the Referee (of the International Match).

13 National Associations, particularly in International Matches, should restrict the number of photographers around the field of play, have a line ('photographers' line') marked behind the goal-lines at least 2 metres from the corner-flag going through a point situated at least 3.5 metres behind the intersection of the goal-line with the line marking the goal area to a point situated at least 6 metres behind the goal-posts, prohibit photographers from passing over these lines and forbid the use of artificial lighting in the form of 'flash-lights'.

14 A mark may be made off the field of play, 11 yards from the corner flag and at right angles to the goal-line, to help the referee ensure that this distance is observed when a corner kick is being taken.

Advice to Referees

Visit the ground in good time before a match to see that everything is in order. If through bad weather or negligence the state of the ground is such that it may endanger the players, refuse to sanction play. If the lines are not properly marked see that, if time allows, it is done before the match.

Examine the goal-nets before every match, ensure that they are properly pegged down and that they are intact.

The Ball

The ball shall be spherical; the outer casing shall be of leather or other suitable materials. No material shall be used in its construction which might prove dangerous to the players. The circumference of the ball shall not be more than 70.0 centimetres and not less than 68.0 centimetres. The weight of the ball at the start of the game shall not be more than 450 grammes nor less than 410 grammes. The pressure shall be equal to 0.6–1.1 atmosphere (= 600–1,100 grammes/centimetres squared) at sea level. The ball shall not be changed during the game unless authorized by the Referee.

INTERNATIONAL BOARD DECISIONS

1 The ball used in any match shall be considered the property of the Association or Club on whose ground the match is played, and at the close of play it must be returned to the Referee.

2 The International Board, from time to time, shall decide what constitutes approved materials. Any approved material shall be certified as such by the International Board.

3 The Board has approved these equivalents of the weights specified in the law:

14 to 16 ounces = 396 to 453 grams.

4 Acceptance of Use

In FIFA competition matches and in competition matches under the auspices of the Confederations, acceptance of a

9

football for use will be conditional upon the football bearing one of the following three designations:

- The official 'FIFA APPROVED' logo, or
- The official 'FIFA INSPECTED' logo or
- The reference 'International Matchball Standard'.

Such designation on a football indicates that it was duly tested and found to be in compliance with the specific technical requirements for each category (FIFA APPROVED, FIFA INSPECTED and International Matchball Standards, the latter being of equal technical standard to FIFA INSPECTED), additional to the minimum specifications set forth in **Law II**. The ball shall carry appropriate indication that it has been successfully tested. Such additional requirements, specific to each of the respective categories, have to be approved by the International F.A. Board. The institutes conducting the tests shall be selected by FIFA.

In all other matches the ball used must satisfy the requirements of **Law II**. National Associations or Competitions may require the use of balls bearing any one of the three aforementioned designations.

5   If the ball bursts or becomes deflated during the course of a match, the game shall be stopped and restarted by dropping the new ball at the place where the first ball became defective, unless it was within the goal-area at that time, in which case it shall be dropped on that part of the goal-area line which runs parallel to the goal-line, at the point nearest to where the ball was when play was stopped.

6   If this happens during a stoppage of the game (place-kick, goal-kick, corner-kick, free-kick, penalty-kick or throw-in) the game shall be restarted accordingly.

Number of Players

(1) A match shall be played by two teams, each consisting of not more than eleven players, one of whom shall be the goalkeeper.

(2) Up to a maximum of three substitutes may be used in any match played in an official competition under the auspices of FIFA, the Confederations, or the National Associations.

The rules of the competition shall state how many substitutes may be nominated, from three up to a maximum of seven.

The names of the substitutes must be given to the Referee prior to the commencement of the match.

Substitutes not so named may not take part in the match.

(3) In other matches, up to five substitutes may also be used provided that the teams concerned reach an agreement on a maximum number, and that the Referee is informed before the match. If the Referee is not informed, or no agreement is reached before the commencement of the match, no more than three substitutes shall be permitted.

The names of the substitutes must be given to the Referee prior to the commencement of the match.

(4) Any of the other players may change places with the goalkeeper, provided that the Referee is informed before the change is made, and provided also that the change is made during a stoppage in the game.

(5) When a goalkeeper or any other player is to be replaced by a substitute, the following conditions shall be observed:–

   (a) the Referee shall be informed of the proposed substitution, before it is made;
   (b) the substitute shall not enter the field of play until the player he is replacing has left, and then only after having received a signal from the Referee;
   (c) he shall enter the field during a stoppage in the game, and at the halfway-line;
   (d) a player who has been replaced shall not take any further part in the game;
   (e) a substitute shall be subject to the authority and jurisdiction of the Referee whether called upon to play or not;
   (f) the substitution is completed when the substitute enters the field of play, from which moment he becomes a player and the player whom he is replacing ceases to be a player.

Punishment

   (a) Play shall not be stopped for an infringement of paragraph 4. The players concerned shall be cautioned immediately the ball goes out of play.
   (b) If a substitute enters the field of play without the authority of the Referee, play shall be stopped. The substitute shall be cautioned and removed from the field or sent off according to the circumstances. The game shall be restarted by the Referee dropping the ball at the place where it was when play was stopped, unless it was within the goal-area at that time, in which case it shall be dropped on that part of the goal-area line which runs parallel to the goal-line, at the point nearest to where the ball was when play was stopped.
   (c) For any other infringement of this Law, the player concerned shall be cautioned, and if the game is stopped by

the Referee to administer the caution, it shall be restarted by an indirect free-kick, to be taken by a player of the opposing team, from the place where the ball was when play was stopped, subject to the over-riding conditions imposed in **Law XIII**.

INTERNATIONAL BOARD DECISIONS

1 The minimum number of players in a team is left to the discretion of National Associations.

2 The Board is of the opinion that a match should not be considered valid if there are fewer than seven players in either of the teams.

3 A player who has been ordered off before play begins may only be replaced by one of the named substitutes. The kick-off must not be delayed to allow the substitute to join his team.

A player who has been ordered off after play has started may not be replaced. A named substitute who has been ordered off, either before or after play has started, may not be replaced. (This decision only relates to players who are ordered off under **Law XII**. It does not apply to players who have infringed **Law IV**.)

Players' Equipment

1 (a) The basic compulsory equipment of a player shall consist of a jersey or shirt, shorts, stockings, shinguards and footwear.

(b) A player shall not wear anything which is dangerous to another player.

2 Shinguards, which must be covered entirely by the stockings, shall be made of a suitable material (rubber, plastic, polyurethane or similar substance) and shall afford a reasonable degree of protection.

3 The goalkeeper shall wear colours which distinguish him from the other players and from the Referee.

Punishment

For any infringement of this Law, the player at fault shall be instructed to leave the field of play by the Referee, to adjust his equipment or obtain any missing equipment, when the ball next ceases to be in play, unless by then the player has already corrected his equipment. Play shall not be stopped immediately for an infringement of this Law. A player who is instructed to leave the field to adjust his equipment or obtain missing equipment shall not return without first reporting to the Referee, who shall satisfy himself that the player's equipment is in order. The player shall only re-enter the game at a moment when the ball has ceased to be in play.

INTERNATIONAL BOARD DECISIONS

1 In International Matches, International Competitions, International Club Competitions and friendly matches between clubs of different National Associations, the Referee, prior to the start of the game, shall inspect the players' equipment, and prevent any player whose equipment does not conform to the requirements of this Law from playing until such time as it does comply.

The rules of any competition may include a similar provision.

2 If the Referee finds that a player is wearing articles not permitted by the Laws and which may constitute a danger to other players, he shall order him to take them off. If he fails to carry out the Referee's instruction, the player shall not take part in the match.

3 A player who has been prevented from taking part in the game or a player who has been sent off the field for infringing **Law IV** must report to the Referee during a stoppage of the game and may not enter or re-enter the field of play unless and until the Referee has satisfied himself that the player is no longer infringing **Law IV**.

4 A player who has been prevented from taking part in a game or who has been sent off because of an infringement of **Law IV**, and who enters or re-enters the field of play to join or rejoin his team in breach of the conditions of **Law XII**(*j*), shall be cautioned.

If the Referee stops the game to administer the caution, the game shall be restarted by an indirect free-kick, taken by a player of the opposing side, from the place where the ball was when the Referee stopped the game, subject to the over-riding conditions imposed in **Law XIII**.

Advice to Referees

Note the implications of International Board Decision No's 1 and 2. Players are regularly reminded that they should ensure that they do not wear any articles (including necklaces and jewellery) which may constitute a danger to other players. Referees are advised strongly to make sure that players do comply so that unnecessary danger is eliminated.

If asked to do so, examine the players' footwear or other equipment before the match or during the interval. If you have any reason for doubt you may require to examine a player's footwear, etc., at any time.

For infringement of this Law there is no need to wait for any appeal; note the offence, which need not be reported.

Referees

A Referee shall be appointed to officiate in each game. His authority and the exercise of the powers granted to him by the Laws of the Game commence as soon as he enters the field of play.

His power of penalizing shall extend to offences committed when play has been temporarily suspended, or when the ball is out of play. His decision on points of fact connected with the play shall be final, so far as the result of the game is concerned.

He shall:–

(a) Enforce the Laws.

(b) Refrain from penalizing in cases where he is satisfied that, by doing so, he would be giving an advantage to the offending team.

(c) Keep a record of the game; act as timekeeper and allow the full or agreed time, adding thereto all time lost through accident or other cause.

(d) Have discretionary power to stop the game for any infringement of the Laws and to suspend or terminate the game whenever, by reasons of the elements, interference by spectators, or other cause, he deems such stoppage necessary. In such a case he shall submit a detailed report to the competent authority, within the stipulated time, and in accordance with the provisions set up by the National Association under whose jurisdiction the match was played.

(e) From the time he enters the field of play, caution and show a yellow card to any player guilty of misconduct or ungentlemanly behaviour. In such cases the Referee shall send the name of the offender to the competent authority, within the stipulated time,* and in accordance with the provisions set up by the National Association under whose jurisdiction the match was played.

(f) Allow no person other than the players and Assistant Referees to enter the field of play without his permission.

(g) Stop the game if, in his opinion, a player has been seriously injured; have the player removed as soon as possible from the field of play, and immediately resume the game. If a player is slightly injured, the game shall not be stopped until the ball has ceased to be in play. A player who is able to go to the touch- or goal-line for attention of any kind shall not be treated on the field of play.

(h) Send off the field of play and show a red card to any player who, in his opinion, is guilty of violent conduct, serious foul play, the use of foul or abusive language, or is guilty of a second cautionable offence.

(i) Signal for recommencement of the game after all stoppages.

(j) Decide that the ball provided for a match meets with the requirements of **Law II**.

INTERNATIONAL BOARD DECISIONS

1 Referees in International Matches shall wear a blazer or blouse the colour of which is distinctive from the colours worn by the contesting teams.

2 Referees for International Matches will be selected from a neutral country unless the countries concerned agree to appoint their own officials.

3 The Referee must be chosen from the official list of Inter-

* In England, within two days. Sunday not included.

national Referees. This need not apply to Amateur and Youth International matches.

4 The Referee shall report to the appropriate authority misconduct or any misdemeanour on the part of spectators, officials, players, named substitutes or other persons which take place either on the field of play or in its vicinity at any time prior to, during, or after the match in question so that appropriate action can be taken by the authority concerned.

5 In no case shall the Referee consider the intervention of an Assistant Referee if he himself has seen the incident and, from his position on the field, is better able to judge. With this reserve, and the Assistant Referee neutral, the Referee can consider the intervention and if the information of the Assistant Referee applies to that phase of the game immediately before the scoring of a goal, the Referee may act thereon and cancel the goal.

6 The Referee, however, can only reverse his first decision so long as the game has not been restarted.

7 If the Referee applies the advantage clause and the advantage which was anticipated does not develop at that time, the referee shall penalise the original offence.

8 The Laws of the Game are intended to provide that games should be played with as little interference as possible, and in this view it is the duty of Referees to penalize only deliberate breaches of the Law. Constant whistling for trifling and doubtful breaches produces bad feeling and loss of temper on the part of the players and spoils the pleasure of spectators.

9 By para. (*d*) of **Law V** the Referee is empowered to terminate a match in the event of grave disorder, but he has no power or right to decide, in such event, that either team is disqualified and thereby the loser of the match. He must send a detailed report to the proper authority who alone has power to deal further with this matter.

10 If a player commits two infringements of a different nature at the same time, the Referee shall punish the more serious offence.

11 It is the duty of the Referee to act upon the information of neutral Assistant Referees with regard to incidents that do not come under the personal notice of the Referee.

12 The Referee shall not allow any person to enter the field of play until play has stopped, and only then if he has given him a signal to do so.

Legal Liability of Referees

13 A Referee (or where applicable an Assistant Referee or Fourth Official) shall not be held liable for (1) any kind of injury suffered by a player, official or spectator, (2) any damage to property of any kind, or (3) any other loss suffered by any individual, club, company, association or similar body, due or which may be due to any decision which he may take in terms of the Laws of the Game or in respect of the normal procedures required to hold, play and control a match.

Such a decision may be –

(a) a decision that the condition of the field of play or its surrounds or that the weather conditions are such as to allow or not to allow a match to take place,

(b) a decision to abandon a match for whatever reason,

(c) a decision as to the condition of the fixtures or equipment used during a match including the goal-posts, cross-bar, corner-posts and the ball,

(d) a decision to stop or not to stop a match due to

spectator interference or any problem in the spectator area,

(e) a decision to stop or not to stop play to allow an injured player to be treated,

(f) a decision to request or insist that an injured player be removed from the field of play for treatment,

(g) a decision to allow or not to allow a player to wear certain apparel or equipment,

(h) a decision (in so far as this may be his responsibility) to allow or not to allow any persons (including team or stadium officials, security officers, photographers or other media representatives) to be present in the vicinity of the field of play,

(i) any other decision which he may take in accordance with the Laws of the Game or in conformity with his duties in terms of the Federation, Association or League Rules or Regulations under which the match is played.

14 The coach may convey tactical instructions to players during the match. The coach and other officials, however, must remain within the confines of the Technical Area,* where such an area is provided and they must conduct themselves, at all times, in a responsible manner.

15 In tournaments or competitions where a Fourth Official† is appointed, his role and duties shall be in accordance with the guide-lines approved by the International Football Association Board.

* see page 54 for details.
† see page 62 for details.

Advice to Referees

To referee in such a way that you will win the respect of players and spectators:–

(a) Learn to understand every Law.

(b) Be absolutely fair and impartial in every decision.

(c) Keep physically fit and in good training.

When considering the suspension or abandonment of a match on account of adverse or deteriorating weather conditions, only make a decision after very careful consideration of all relevant factors.

When cautioning a player, state he is being cautioned and inquire his name, and that if he persists in misconduct after having received a Caution, he will be ordered off the field. The Referee will only show the yellow card after this procedure has been completed.

If a player is to be sent off for a second cautionable offence in a match, the Referee is required to show first the yellow card and immediately afterwards the red card (thus making it obvious that the player is being sent off because of a second cautionable offence and not because of an offence requiring immediate expulsion). For a single offence requiring an immediate expulsion, only the red card is shown after the standard procedure.

Note the procedure if a player is cautioned; a Referee who fails to report misconduct which came under his notice may be suspended, if it is proved to the satisfaction of the Council that the case of misconduct should have been further investigated.

Compare watches with the Assistant Referees, both before the game and at half-time.

Do not trust to memory alone in keeping a record of the game; note the time of start and the time at which, if no time has to be allowed for stoppages, half-time and the end of the game will fall due. Note also the goals as they are scored.

The application of the provisions of (g) should be strictly

observed. Referees should be concerned about the welfare of players in their application of this section and are reminded of the need for a rapid assessment and to stop play when a serious injury and/or head injury occurs; they must be vigilant and err on the side of caution in such cases. Care needs to be exercised before a seriously injured player is removed from the field of play – continue to err on the side of safety – and accept the advice of those who are medically qualified or claim to have such similar skills.

Registered Referees are not permitted to officiate in unsanctioned matches or competitions.

Assistant Referees

Two Assistant Referees shall be appointed, whose duty (subject to the decision of the Referee) shall be to indicate:

(a) when the ball is out of play;
(b) which side is entitled to a corner-kick, goal-kick or throw-in;
(c) when a player may be penalised for being in an offside position;
(d) when misconduct or other incident has occurred out of the vision of the referee;
(e) when a substitution is desired.

They shall also assist the Referee to control the game in accordance with the Laws. In the event of undue interference or improper conduct by an Assistant Referee, the Referee shall dispense with his services and arrange for a substitute to be appointed. (The matter shall be reported by the Referee to the competent authority.) The Assistant Referee should be equipped with flags by the Club on whose ground the match is played.

INTERNATIONAL BOARD DECISIONS

1 Assistant Referees where neutral shall draw the Referee's attention to any breach of the Laws of the Game of which they become aware if they consider that the Referee may not have seen it, but the Referee shall always be the judge of the decision to be taken.

2 In International 'A' Matches, National Associations should appoint Neutral Assistant Referees from the International List.

3 In International Matches, Assistant Referees' flags shall be of a vivid colour – bright reds and yellows. Such flags are recommended for use in all other matches.

4 An Assistant Referee may be subject to disciplinary action only upon a report of the Referee for unjustified interference or insufficient assistance.

Advice to Referees

To prevent being touched by the ball or interfering with play, Assistant Referees should, as far as possible, keep out of the field of play.

Duration of the Game

The duration of the game shall be two equal periods of 45 minutes, unless otherwise mutually agreed upon, subject to the following:–

(a) Allowance shall be made in either period for all time lost through substitution, the transport from the field of injured players, time-wasting or other cause, the amount of which shall be a matter for the discretion of the Referee.

(b) Time shall be extended to permit of a penalty-kick being taken at or after the expiration of the normal period in either half.

The half-time interval shall not exceed fifteen minutes.

Competition rules shall clearly stipulate the duration of the half-time interval.

The duration of the half-time interval may be altered only with the consent of the referee.

INTERNATIONAL BOARD DECISIONS

1 If a match has been stopped by the Referee, before the completion of the time specified in the rules, for any reason stated in **Law V** it must be replayed in full unless the rules of the competition concerned provide for the result of the match at the time of such stoppage to stand.

2 Players have a right to an interval at half-time.

Advice to Referees

A Referee has no power to set aside the Rules of Cup and other Competitions where the time to be played is specified. It is essential that Referees are aware of precise details of Competition Rules, e.g. number of substitutions permitted to be nominated, method of deciding the outcome of drawn matches.

Normal period means 90 minutes, or if a shorter period is mutually agreed upon and is permissible under the Rules of the Competition the period should be divided in equal halves.

The Start of Play

(a) **At the beginning of the game**, choice of ends and the kick-off shall be decided by the toss of a coin. The team winning the toss shall have the option of choice of ends or the kick-off.

The Referee having given a signal, the game shall be started by a player taking a place-kick (i.e., a kick at the ball while it is stationary on the ground in the centre of the field of play) into his opponents' half of the field of play. Every player shall be in his own half of the field and every player of the team opposing that of the kicker shall remain not less than 10 yards from the ball until it is kicked-off; it shall not be deemed in play until it has travelled the distance of its own circumference. The kicker shall not play the ball a second time until it has been touched or played by another player.

(b) **After a goal has been scored**, the game shall be restarted in like manner by a player of the team losing the goal.

(c) **After half-time**: when restarting after half-time, ends shall be changed and the kick-off shall be taken by a player of the opposite team to that of the player who started the game.

Punishment

For any infringement of this Law, the kick-off shall be retaken, except in the case of the kicker playing the ball again before it has been touched or played by another player; for this offence, an indirect free-kick shall be taken by a player of the opposing team from the place where the infringement occurred, subject to the over-riding conditions imposed in **Law XIII**.

A goal shall not be scored direct from a kick-off.

(d) **After any other temporary suspension**: when restarting the game after a temporary suspension of play from any cause not mentioned elsewhere in these Laws, provided that immediately prior to the suspension the ball has not passed over the touch- or goal-lines, the Referee shall drop the ball at the place where it was when play was suspended, unless it was within the goal-area at that time, in which case it shall be dropped on that part of the goal-area line which runs parallel to the goal-line, at the point nearest to where the ball was when play was stopped. It shall be deemed in play when it has touched the ground; if, however, it goes over the touch- or goal-lines after it has been dropped by the Referee, but before it is touched by a player, the Referee shall again drop it. A player shall not play the ball until it has touched the ground. If this section of the Law is not complied with the Referee shall again drop the ball.

INTERNATIONAL BOARD DECISIONS

1 If, when the Referee drops the ball, a player infringes any of the Laws before the ball has touched the ground, the player concerned shall be cautioned or sent off the field according to the seriousness of the offence, but a free-kick cannot be awarded to the opposing team because the ball was not in play at the time of the offence. The ball shall therefore be again dropped by the Referee.

2 Kicking-off by persons other than the players competing in a match is prohibited.

Advice to Referees

Note which side kicks off; the kick must be taken by a player competing in the match.

When extra time is necessary, play shall be restarted according to **Law VIII** (a). The interval between the end of the normal period of play and the start of the extra period shall be under the jurisdiction of the Referee.

Ball In and Out of Play

The ball is out of play:–

- (a) When it has wholly crossed the goal-line or touch-line, whether on the ground or in the air.
- (b) When the game has been stopped by the Referee.

The ball is in play at all other times from the start of the match to the finish including:–

- (a) If it rebounds from a goal-post, cross-bar or corner-flag post into the field of play.
- (b) If it rebounds off either the Referee or Assistant Referees when they are in the field of play.
- (c) In the event of a supposed infringement of the Laws, until a decision is given.

INTERNATIONAL BOARD DECISIONS

1 The lines belong to the areas of which they are the boundaries. In consequence, the touch-lines and the goal-lines belong to the field of play.

Method of Scoring

Except as otherwise provided by these Laws, a goal is scored when the whole of the ball has passed over the goal-line, between the goal-posts and under the cross-bar, provided it has not been thrown, carried or intentionally propelled by hand or arm, by a player of the attacking side, except in the case of a goalkeeper, who is within his own penalty area.

The team scoring the greater number of goals during a game shall be the winner; if no goals, or an equal number of goals are scored, the game shall be termed a 'draw'.

INTERNATIONAL BOARD DECISIONS

1 Law X defines the only method according to which a match is won or drawn; no variation whatsoever can be authorized.

2 A goal cannot in any case be allowed if the ball has been prevented by some outside agent from passing over the goal-line. If this happens in the normal course of play, other than at the taking of a penalty-kick, the game must be stopped and restarted by the Referee dropping the ball at the place where the ball came into contact with the interference, unless it was within the goal-area at that time, in which case it shall be dropped on that part of the goal-area line which runs parallel to the goal-line, at the point nearest to where the ball was when play was stopped.

3 If, when the ball is going into goal, a spectator enters the field before it passes wholly over the goal-line, and tries to prevent a score, a goal shall be allowed if the ball goes into goal, unless the spectator has made contact with the ball or has interfered with play, in which case the Referee shall stop the game and restart it by dropping the ball at the place where the contact or interference occurred, unless it was within the goal-area at that time, in which case it shall be dropped on that part of the goal-area line which runs parallel to the goal-line, at the point nearest to where the ball was when play was stopped.

Off-Side

(1) A player is in an off-side position if he is nearer to his opponents' goal-line than the ball, unless:

    (a) he is in his own half of the field of play, or
    (b) he is not nearer to his opponents' goal-line than at least two of his opponents.

(2) **It is not an offence in itself to be in an off-side position.**
A player shall only be penalised for being in an off-side position if, at the moment the ball touches, or is played by one of his team, he is, **in the opinion of the Referee, involved in active play by**:

    (a) interfering with play, or
    (b) interfering with an opponent, or
    (c) gaining an advantage by being in that position.

(3) A player shall not be declared off-side by the Referee

    (a) merely because of his being in an off-side position, or
    (b) if he receives the ball, direct from a goal-kick, a corner-kick, or a throw-in.

(4) If a player is declared off-side, the Referee shall award an indirect free-kick, which shall be taken by a player of the opposing team from the place where the infringement occurred, unless the offence is committed by a player in his opponents' goal-area, in which case the free-kick shall be taken from any point within the goal-area.

INTERNATIONAL BOARD DECISIONS

1   Off-side shall not be judged at the moment the player in question receives the ball, but at the moment when the ball is passed to him by one of his own side. A player who is not in an off-side position when one of his colleagues passes the ball to him or takes a free-kick, does not therefore become off-side if he goes forward during the flight of the ball.

2   A player who is level with the second last opponent or with the last two opponents is not in an off-side position.

Fouls and Misconduct

A player who commits any of the following six offences in a manner considered by the Referee to be careless, reckless or involving disproportionate force:

(a) kicks or attempts to kick an opponent; or
(b) trips an opponent; or
(c) jumps at an opponent; or
(d) charges an opponent; or
(e) strikes or attempts to strike an opponent; or
(f) pushes an opponent;

or who commits any of the following four offences:

(g) when tackling an opponent makes contact with the opponent before contact is made with the ball; or
(h) holds an opponent or
spits at an opponent; or
(i) handles the ball deliberately, i.e., carries, strikes or propels the ball with his hand or arm (this does not apply to the goalkeeper within his own penalty-area);

shall be penalized by the award of a **direct free-kick** to be taken by the opposing team from the place where the offence occurred, unless the offence is committed by a player in his opponents' goal-area, in which case the free-kick shall be taken from any point within the goal-area.

Should a player of the defending team commit one of the above ten offences within the penalty-area, he shall be penalized by a **penalty-kick**.

A penalty-kick can be awarded irrespective of the position of the ball, if in play, at the time an offence within the penalty-area is committed.

A player committing any of the five following offences:–

1 playing in a manner considered by the Referee to be dangerous;

2 charging fairly, i.e. with the shoulder, when the ball is not within playing distance of the players concerned and they are definitely not trying to play it;

3 when not playing the ball, impeding the progress of an opponent, i.e. running between the opponent and the ball, or interposing the body so as to form an obstacle to an opponent;

4 charging the goalkeeper except when he:–

(a) is holding the ball;
(b) is obstructing an opponent;
(c) has passed outside his goal-area;

5 when playing as a goalkeeper and within his own penalty-area:–

(a) from the moment he takes control of the ball with his hands, he takes more than 4 steps in any direction whilst holding, bouncing or throwing the ball in the air and catching it again, without releasing it into play, or

(b) having released the ball into play before, during or after the 4 steps, he touches it again with his hands, before it has been touched or played by a player of the opposing team either inside or outside of the penalty-area, or by a player of the same team outside the penalty-area, subject to the over-riding conditions of 5(c), or

(c) touches the ball with his hands after it has been deliberately kicked to him by a team-mate, or

(d) indulges in tactics which, in the opinion of the Referee, are designed merely to hold up the game and thus waste time and so give an unfair advantage to his own team,

shall be penalized by the award of an **indirect free-kick** to be taken by the opposing side from the place where the infringement occurred, subject to the over-riding conditions imposed in **Law XIII**.

A player shall be **cautioned** and shown the yellow card if:–

(j) he enters or re-enters the field of play to join or re-join his team after the game has commenced, or leaves the field of play during the progress of the game (except through accident) without, in either case, first having received a signal from the Referee showing him that he may do so. If the Referee stops the game to administer the caution, the game shall be restarted by an indirect free-kick taken by a player of the opposing team from the place where the ball was when the Referee stopped the game, subject to the over-riding conditions imposed in **Law XIII**.

If, however, the offending player has committed a more serious offence, he shall be penalized according to that section of the law he infringed;

(k) he persistently infringes the Laws of the Game;

(l) he shows, by word or action, dissent from any decision given by the Referee;

(m) he is guilty of ungentlemanly conduct.

For any of these last three offences, in addition to the caution an **indirect free-kick** shall be awarded to the opposing side from the place where the offence occurred, subject to the over-riding conditions imposed in **Law XIII**, unless a more serious infringement of the Laws of the Game was committed.

A player shall be sent off the field of play and shown the red card if, in the opinion of the Referee, he:–

(n) is guilty of violent conduct;
(o) is guilty of serious foul play;
(p) uses foul or abusive language;
(q) is guilty of a second cautionable offence after having received a caution.

If play is stopped by reason of a player being ordered from the field for an offence without a separate breach of the Law having been committed, the game shall be resumed by an **indirect free-kick** awarded to the opposing side from the place where the infringement occurred, subject to the over-riding conditions imposed in **Law XIII**.

INTERNATIONAL BOARD DECISIONS

1 If the goalkeeper either strikes an opponent by throwing the ball at him or pushes him with the ball while still holding it, the Referee shall award a penalty kick if the offence took place within the penalty area.

2 If a player leans on the shoulders of another player of his own team in order to head the ball, the Referee shall stop the game, caution the player for ungentlemanly conduct and award an indirect free-kick to the opposing side.

3 A player's obligation when joining or rejoining his team after the start of the match to 'report to the Referee' must be interpreted as meaning to 'draw the attention of the Referee from the touch-line'. The signal from the Referee shall be made by a definite gesture which makes the player understand that he may come into the field of play; it is not necessary for the Referee to wait until the game is stopped (this does not apply in respect of an infringement of **Law IV**), but the Referee is the sole judge of the moment in which he gives his signal of acknowledgement.

4   The letter and spirit of **Law XII** do not oblige the Referee to stop a game to administer a caution. He may, if he chooses, apply the advantage. If he does apply the advantage, he shall caution the player when play stops.

5   If a player covers up the ball without touching it in an endeavour not to have it played by an opponent, he obstructs but does not infringe **Law XII**, para. 3, because he is already in possession of the ball and covers it for tactical reasons whilst the ball remains within playing distance. In fact, he is actually playing the ball and does not commit an infringement; in this case, the player may be charged because he is in fact playing the ball.

6   If a player positions his arms to impede an opponent and steps from one side to the other, moving his arms up and down to delay his opponent, forcing him to change course, but does not make 'bodily contact', the referee shall caution the player for ungentlemanly conduct and award an indirect free-kick.

7   If a player impedes the progress of the opposing goalkeeper, in an attempt to prevent him from playing the ball in accordance with **Law XII**, 5(a), the referee shall award an indirect free-kick.

8   If after a Referee has awarded a free-kick a player protests violently by using abusive or foul language and is sent off the field, the free-kick should not be taken until the player has left the field.

9   Any player, whether he is within or outside the field of play, whose conduct is ungentlemanly or violent, whether or not it is directed towards an opponent, a colleague, the Referee, an Assistant Referee or other person, or who uses foul or abusive language, is guilty of an offence, and shall be dealt with according to the nature of the offence committed.

10 If, in the opinion of the Referee, a goalkeeper lies on the ball longer than is necessary, he shall be penalized for ungentlemanly conduct and

(a) be cautioned, and an indirect free-kick awarded to the opposing team;

(b) in case of repetition of the offence, be sent off the field.

11 The offence of spitting at officials or other persons, or similar unseemly behaviour, shall be considered as violent conduct within the meaning of section (n) of **Law XII**.

12 If, when a Referee is about to caution a player, and before he has done so, the player commits another offence which merits a caution, the player shall be sent off the field of play.

13 If, in the opinion of the Referee, a player who is moving toward his opponent's goal with an obvious opportunity to score a goal is impeded by an opponent, through unlawful means, i.e. an offence punishable by a free-kick (or a penalty-kick), thus denying the attacking player's team the aforesaid goal-scoring opportunity, the offending player shall be sent off the field of play for serious foul play in accordance with **Law XII**(o).

14 If, in the opinion of the Referee, a player, other than the goalkeeper within his own penalty-area, denies his opponents a goal, or an obvious goal-scoring opportunity, by intentionally handling the ball, he shall be sent off the field of play for serious foul play in accordance with **Law XII**(o).

15 The International F.A. Board is of the opinion that a goalkeeper, in the circumstances described in **Law XII**, 5(a), will be considered to be in control of the ball when he takes possession of the ball by touching it with any part of his hands or arms. Possession of the ball would include the goalkeeper intentionally parrying the ball, but would not include the circumstances where, in the opinion of the Referee, the ball rebounds accidentally from the goalkeeper, for example after he has made a save.

16 Subject to the terms of **Law XII**, a player may pass the ball to his own goalkeeper using his head or chest or knee, etc. If, however, in the opinion of the Referee, a player uses a deliberate trick in order to circumvent article 5(c) of **Law XII**, the player will be guilty of ungentlemanly conduct and will be punished accordingly under the terms of **Law XII**; that is to say, the player will be cautioned and shown the yellow card and an indirect free-kick will be awarded to the opposing team from the place where the player committed the offence.

In such circumstances, it is irrelevant whether the goalkeeper subsequently touches the ball with his hands or not. The offence is committed by the player in attempting to circumvent both the text and the spirit of **Law XII**.

Advice to Referees

A thorough knowledge of this Law is absolutely essential, but its correct application depends on the Referee's ability to make up his mind whether or not a player's action in connection with (a) to (f) should be considered to have been made in a CARELESS OR RECKLESS manner, or whether it has been committed with an excessive amount of force.

Although an opponent is entitled to make a fair charge on the goalkeeper when he is holding the ball in his hands, it is not then permissible for an opponent to attempt to kick the ball.

Free-Kick

Free-kicks shall be classified under two headings: 'Direct' (from which a goal can be scored direct against the **offending side**), and 'Indirect' (from which a goal cannot be scored unless the ball has been played or touched by a player other than the kicker before passing through the goal).

When a player is taking a direct or an indirect free-kick inside his own penalty-area, all of the opposing players shall be at least 10 yards (9.15 m) from the ball and shall remain outside the penalty-area until the ball has been kicked out of the area. The ball shall be in play immediately it has travelled the distance of its own circumference and is beyond the penalty-area. The goalkeeper shall not receive the ball into his hands, in order that he may thereafter kick it into play. If the ball is not kicked direct into play, beyond the penalty-area, the kick shall be retaken.

When a player is taking a direct or an indirect free-kick outside his own penalty-area, all of the opposing players shall be at least 10 yards from the ball, until it is in play, unless they are standing on their own goal-line, between the goal-posts. The ball shall be in play when it has travelled the distance of its own circumference.

If a player of the opposing side encroaches into the penalty-area, or within 10 yards of the ball, as the case may be, before a free-kick is taken, the Referee shall delay the taking of the kick, until the Law is complied with.

The ball must be stationary when a free-kick is taken, and the kicker shall not play the ball a second time, until it has been touched or played by another player.

Notwithstanding any other reference in these Laws to the point from which a free-kick is to be taken:

1 Any free-kick awarded to the defending team, within its own goal-area, may be taken from any point within the goal-area.

2   Any indirect free-kick awarded to the attacking team within its opponent's goal-area shall be taken from the part of the goal-area line which runs parallel to the goal-line, at the point nearest to where the offence was committed.

Punishment

If the kicker, after taking the free-kick, plays the ball a second time before it has been touched or played by another player an indirect free-kick shall be taken by a player of the opposing team from the spot where the infringement occurred, unless the offence is committed by a player in his opponents' goal-area, in which case the free-kick shall be taken from any point within the goal-area.

INTERNATIONAL BOARD DECISIONS

1   In order to distinguish between a direct and an indirect free-kick, the Referee, when he awards an indirect free-kick, shall indicate accordingly by raising an arm above his head. He shall keep his arm in that position until the kick has been taken and retain the signal until the ball has been played or touched by another player or goes out of play.

2   Players who do not retire to the proper distance when a free-kick is taken must be cautioned and on any repetition be ordered off. It is particularly requested of Referees that attempts to delay the taking of a free-kick by encroaching should be treated as serious misconduct.

3   If, when a free-kick is being taken, any of the players dance about or gesticulate in a way calculated to distract their opponents, it shall be deemed ungentlemanly conduct for which the offender(s) shall be cautioned.

Advice to Referees

If a player kicks the ball directly into his own goal from a direct or indirect free-kick, the Referee should award a corner-kick provided that in the case of a free-kick inside the penalty-area the ball had first been kicked into play. In this context any free-kick incorrectly taken from inside the penalty-area must be retaken. When a player kicks the ball directly into his opponents' goal from an indirect free-kick, the Referee should award a goal-kick to the opponents.

Penalty-Kick

A penalty-kick shall be taken from the penalty-mark and, when it is being taken, all players with the exception of the player taking the kick, properly identified, and the opposing goalkeeper, shall be within the field of play but outside the penalty-area, at least 10 yards from the penalty-mark **and must stand behind the penalty mark**.

The opposing goalkeeper must stand (without moving his feet) on his own goal-line, between the goal-posts, until the ball is kicked. The player taking the kick must kick the ball forward; he shall not play the ball a second time until it has been touched or played by another player. The ball shall be deemed in play directly it is kicked, i.e., when it has travelled the distance of its circumference. A goal may be scored directly from a penalty-kick. When a penalty-kick is being taken during the normal course of play, or when time has been extended at half-time or full-time to allow a penalty-kick to be taken or retaken, a goal shall not be nullified if, before passing between the posts and under the cross-bar, the ball touches either or both of the goal-posts, or the cross-bar, or the goalkeeper, or any combination of these agencies, providing that no other infringement has occurred.

Punishment

For any infringement of this Law:

(a) by the defending team, the kick shall be retaken if a goal has not resulted;

(b) by the attacking team, other than by the player taking the kick, if a goal is scored it shall be disallowed and the kick retaken;

(c) by the player taking the penalty-kick, committed after the ball is in play, a player of the opposing team shall take an indirect free-kick from the spot where the infringement occurred, subject to the over-riding conditions imposed in **Law XIII**.

INTERNATIONAL BOARD DECISIONS

1 When the Referee has awarded a penalty-kick, he shall not signal for it to be taken until the players have taken up position in accordance with the Law.

2 (a) If, after the kick has been taken, the ball is stopped in its course towards goal by an outside agent, the kick shall be retaken.

  (b) If, after the kick has been taken, the ball rebounds into play, from the goalkeeper, the cross-bar or a goal-post, and is then stopped in its course by an outside agent, the Referee shall stop play and restart it by dropping the ball at the place where it came into contact with the outside agent, unless it was within the goal-area at that time, in which case it shall be dropped on that part of the goal-area line which runs parallel to the goal-line, at the point nearest to where the ball was when play was stopped.

3 (a) If, after having given the signal for a penalty-kick to be taken, the Referee sees that the goalkeeper is not in his right place on the goal-line, he shall, nevertheless, allow the kick to proceed. It shall be retaken if a goal is not scored.

  (b) If, after the Referee has given the signal for the penalty-kick to be taken, and before the ball has been kicked, the goalkeeper moves his feet, the Referee shall, nevertheless, allow the kick to proceed. It shall be retaken if a goal is not scored.

  (c) If, after the Referee has given the signal for a penalty-kick to be taken, and before the ball is in play, a player of the defending team encroaches into the penalty-area, or within 10 yards of the penalty-mark, the Referee shall, nevertheless, allow the kick to proceed. It shall be retaken if a goal is not scored.

The player concerned shall be cautioned.

4 (a) If, when a penalty-kick is being taken, the player taking the kick is guilty of ungentlemanly conduct, the kick, if already taken shall be retaken, if a goal is scored.

The player concerned shall be cautioned.

(b) If, after the Referee has given the signal for a penalty-kick to be taken, and before the ball is in play, a colleague of the player taking the kick encroaches into the penalty-area or within 10 yards of the penalty-mark, the Referee shall, nevertheless, allow the kick to proceed. If a goal is scored, it shall be disallowed, and the kick retaken.

The player concerned shall be cautioned.

(c) If, in the circumstances described in the foregoing paragraph, the ball rebounds into play from the goalkeeper, the cross-bar or a goal-post, and a goal has not been scored, the Referee shall stop the game, caution the player and award an indirect free-kick to the opposing team from the place where the infringement occurred, subject to the over-riding conditions imposed in **Law XIII**.

5 (a) If, after the Referee has given the signal for a penalty-kick to be taken, and before the ball is in play, the goalkeeper moves from his position on the goal-line, or moves his feet, and a colleague of the kicker encroaches into the penalty-area or within 10 yards of the penalty-mark, the kick, if taken, shall be retaken.

The colleague of the kicker shall be cautioned.

(b) If, after the Referee has given the signal for a penalty-kick to be taken, and before the ball is in play, a player of each team encroaches into the penalty-area, or within 10 yards of the penalty-mark, the kick, if taken, shall be retaken.

The players concerned shall be cautioned.

6   When a match is extended, at half-time or full-time, to allow a penalty-kick to be taken or retaken, the extension shall last until the moment that the penalty-kick has been completed, i.e., until the Referee has decided whether or not a goal is scored, and the game shall terminate immediately the Referee has made his decision.

After the player taking the penalty-kick has put the ball into play, no player other than the defending goalkeeper may play or touch the ball before the kick is completed.

7   When a penalty-kick is being taken in extended time:–

   (a)   the provisions of all the foregoing paragraphs, except paragraphs 2 (b) and 4 (c) shall apply in the usual way, and

   (b)   in the circumstances described in paragraphs 2 (b) and 4 (c) the game shall terminate immediately the ball rebounds from the goalkeeper, the cross-bar or the goal-post.

Advice to Referees

If the original offence was sufficiently serious to justify the offender being sent from the field of play, the penalty-kick alone is not sufficient punishment. If the ball hits a goal-post or the cross-bar and rebounds into play, the player taking the penalty-kick must not play it again until it has been touched by another player.

Throw-In

When the whole of the ball passes over the touch-line, either on the ground or in the air, it shall be thrown in from the point where it crossed the line, in any direction, by a player of the team opposite to that of the player who last touched it. The thrower at the moment of delivering the ball must face the field of play and part of each foot shall be either on the touch-line or on the ground outside the touch-line. The thrower shall use both hands and shall deliver the ball from behind and over his head. The ball shall be in play immediately it enters the field of play, but the thrower shall not again play the ball until it has been touched or played by another player. A goal shall not be scored direct from a throw-in.

Punishment

(a) If the ball is improperly thrown in the throw-in shall be taken by a player of the opposing team.

(b) If the thrower plays the ball a second time before it has been touched or played by another player, an indirect free-kick shall be taken by a player of the opposing team from the place where the infringement occurred, subject to the over-riding conditions imposed in **Law XIII**.

INTERNATIONAL BOARD DECISIONS

1 If a player taking a throw-in, plays the ball a second time by handling it within the field of play before it has been touched or played by another player, the Referee shall award a direct free-kick.

2 A player taking a throw-in must face the field of play with some part of his body.

3 If, when a throw-in is being taken, any of the opposing players dance about or gesticulate in a way calculated to distract or impede the thrower, it shall be deemed ungentlemanly conduct, for which the offender(s) shall be cautioned.

4 A throw-in taken from any position other than the point where the ball passed over the touch-line shall be considered to have been improperly thrown in.

Advice to Referees

When a ball is thrown by a player directly from a throw-in into his opponents' goal, the Referee should award a goal-kick. If, however, a player throws the ball directly into his own goal, the Referee should award a corner-kick.

Goal-Kick

When the whole of the ball passes over the goal-line excluding that portion between the goal-posts, either in the air or on the ground, having last been played by one of the attacking team, it shall be kicked direct into play beyond the penalty-area from any point within the goal-area, by a player of the defending team. A goalkeeper shall not receive the ball into his hands from a goal-kick in order that he may thereafter kick it into play. If the ball is not kicked beyond the penalty-area, i.e., direct into play, the kick shall be retaken. The kicker shall not play the ball a second time until it has touched or been played by another player. A goal shall not be scored direct from such a kick. Players of the team opposing that of the player taking the goal-kick shall remain outside the penalty-area until the ball has been kicked out of the penalty-area.

Punishment

If a player taking a goal-kick plays the ball a second time after it has passed beyond the penalty-area, but before it has touched or been played by another player, an indirect free-kick shall be awarded to the opposing team, to be taken from the place where the infringement occurred, subject to the over-riding conditions imposed in **Law XIII**.

INTERNATIONAL BOARD DECISIONS

1 When a goal-kick has been taken and the player who has kicked the ball touches it again before it has left the penalty-area, the kick has not been taken in accordance with the Law and must be retaken.

Advice to Referees

Before giving the signal for the kick, make sure that the player
and the ball are correctly positioned.

ay On – Advantage. Where the
feree sees an offence but uses the
dvantage, he shall indicate that play
all continue

direct Free-kick. This signal shall
maintained until the kick has been
ken and retained until the ball has
en played or touched by another
ayer or goes out of play

Direct Free-kick. The hand and arm clearly indicate the direction

Penalty-kick. The referee clearly indicates the penalty-mark, but there is no need to run towards it

Goal-kick

Corner-kick

Caution or Expulsion. With the card system in operation, the card shall be shown in the manner illustrated. The player's identity *must* be recorded at the time

Off-side. Flag held upright to indicate Off-side

Off-side. When the referee stops play,
assistant referee indicates position of
...side of the field

Off-side. Position on near side of the
field

Off-side. Position near the centre the field

Throw-in

Back view of the assistant referee signalling to the referee for a substitution to be made

Front view of the assistant referee signalling to the referee when a substitute is waiting at the touch-line

Corner-kick. The assistant referee may first need to signal that the ball has gone o
of play if there is any doubt. He should also look at the referee in case he has alrea
made his own decision which may be different from the assistant referee's

Goal-kick

Corner-Kick

When the whole of the ball passes over the goal-line, excluding that portion between the goal-posts, either in the air or on the ground, having last been played by one of the defending team, a member of the attacking team shall take a corner-kick, i.e., the whole of the ball shall be placed within the quarter circle at the nearest corner flag-post, which must not be moved, and it shall be kicked from that position.

A goal may be scored direct from such a kick. Players of the team opposing that of the player taking the corner-kick shall not approach within 10 yards of the ball until it is in play, i.e., it has travelled the distance of its own circumference, nor shall the kicker play the ball a second time until it has been touched or played by another player.

Punishment

(a) If the player who takes the kick plays the ball a second time before it has been touched or played by another player, the Referee shall award an indirect free-kick to the opposing team, to be taken from the place where the infringement occurred, subject to the over-riding conditions imposed in **Law XIII**.

(b) For any other infringement the kick shall be retaken.

Advice to Referees

If a player, before taking a corner-kick, removes the corner flag-post, order it to be replaced before giving the signal for the corner-kick to be taken.

The Technical Area

The Technical Area as defined in **Law V**, International F.A. Board Decision No. 14, relates particularly to matches played in stadia with a designated seated area for technical staff and substitutes.

It is recognized that Technical Areas may vary between stadia, for example in size or location, but notwithstanding, the following notes are issued for general guidance.

1   The Technical Area shall be considered as extending 1 metre on either side of the designated seated area and shall extend forward up to a distance of 1 metre away from the touchline.

2   It is recommended that markings be used to define this area.

3   The number of persons permitted to occupy the Technical Area shall be defined by the rules of the competition.

4   The occupants of the Technical Area shall be identified before the commencement of the match in accordance with the rules of the competition.

5   Only one person has the authority to convey technical instructions and he must return to his position immediately after giving these instructions.

6   The Coach and other officials must remain within the confines of the Technical Area except in special circumstances, for example, a physiotherapist or doctor entering the field of play with the referee's permission to treat an injured player.

7   The Coach and other occupants of the Technical Area must conduct themselves, at all times, in a responsible manner.

Kicks from the Penalty Mark

Procedures and Check-list for Referees

The International Board at its Meeting on 27th June 1970 accepted a proposal by The Fédération Internationale de Football Association that the practice of drawing lots to determine which of two teams in a drawn match should proceed to a later stage of a Knock-Out Competition or receive the trophy (if any) be discontinued and be replaced by the taking of kicks from the penalty mark which shall not be considered part of the match, subject to the following conditions:–

1   The Referee shall choose the goal at which all of the kicks shall be taken.

2   He shall toss a coin, and the team whose captain wins the toss shall take the first kick.

3   The Referee will record the names of the players who have taken the kicks from the penalty mark, in order to ensure that the provisions of paragraph 7, below, are adhered to.

4   (a)   Subject to the terms of the following paragraphs (c) and (d) both teams shall take five kicks.
   (b)   The kicks shall be taken alternately.
   (c)   If, before both teams have taken five kicks, one has scored more goals than the other could, even if it were to complete its five kicks, the taking of kicks shall cease.
   (d)   If, after both teams have taken five kicks, both have scored the same number of goals, or have not scored any goals, the taking of kicks shall continue in the same order, until

such time as both have taken an equal number of kicks (not necessarily five more kicks) and one has scored a goal more than the other.

5 The team which scores the greater number of goals, whether the number of kicks taken is in accordance with the terms of the foregoing paragraph 4(a), 4(c) or 4(d) shall qualify for the next round of the competition, or shall be declared winner of the competition, as the case may be.

6 (a) With the exception referred to in the following paragraph (b) only the players who are on the field of play at the end of the match, which shall mean at the end of extra time in so far as a match in which extra time is authorized is concerned, and any who, having left the field temporarily, with or without the Referee's permission, are not on the field of play at that time, shall take part in the taking of the kicks.

(b) Provided that his team has not already made use of the maximum number of substitutes permitted by the rules of the competition under which the match was played, a goalkeeper who sustains an injury during the taking of the kicks, and who, because of the injury, is unable to continue as goalkeeper may be replaced by a substitute.

7 Each kick shall be taken by a different player, and not until all eligible players of any team, including the goalkeeper or the named substitute by whom he was replaced in terms of paragraph 6 as the case may be, have each taken a kick may a player of the same team take a second kick.

8 Subject to the terms of paragraph 6 any player who is eligible may change places with his goalkeeper at any time during the taking of the kicks.

9 (a) Other than the player taking a kick from the penalty mark, and the two goalkeepers, all players shall remain within the centre circle whilst the taking of kicks is in progress.

(b) The goalkeeper who is a colleague of the kicker, shall take up position within the field of play, outside the penalty area at which the kicks are being taken, behind the line which runs parallel with the goal-line, and at least 10 yards from the penalty mark.

10 Unless stated to the contrary in the foregoing paragraphs 1 to 9, the Laws of the Game, and the International Board Decisions relating thereto, shall, in so far as they can, apply at the taking of the kicks.

N.B. In the event of light failing before the end of the taking of kicks from the penalty mark, the result shall be decided by the toss of a coin or the drawing of lots.

Check-list for Referees

1 Decide at which end the kicks will be taken. This can be an important decision if the supporters of one team are behind one goal and those of the other team are at the opposite goal.

2 The team which wins the toss must take the first kick.

3 Before the kicks begin, ensure that all club officials, etc., have left the field and that only the players are left.

4 Make sure all players, apart from the kicker and the two goalkeepers, are inside the centre circle.

5 Make sure the goalkeeper of the kicker's team stands outside the penalty area, in the position shown in the diagram.

6 The Laws of the Game, particularly **Law XIV** 'The Penalty-Kick', apply except where modified by the instructions for the taking of kicks from the penalty mark. Be particularly vigilant therefore for instances of gamesmanship or for infringements by the goalkeeper, e.g. moving before the ball is kicked.

7 Keep a careful record of the kicks taken.

8 Where you have the assistance of Assistant Referees some of those duties may be taken by them, e.g. an Assistant Referee at the centre circle would organize players coming to take the kick while the other Assistant Referee would assist by indicating whether or not the ball has crossed the goal-line.

9 It is very important that the referee organizes the taking of kicks from the penalty mark correctly. Make sure you fully understand the instructions.

10 The taking of kicks from the penalty mark never forms part of an actual match. It is only a method of deciding a winner.

11 If, at the taking of kicks from the penalty mark, the light fails badly and the kicks therefore cannot be completed, the result shall be decided by the tossing of a coin or the drawing of lots.

12 An injured player may be excused from the taking of kicks from the penalty mark.

13 It is the responsibility of each team to select the players who will take the kicks from the penalty mark. The Referee's only duty is to ensure that they are taken correctly.

14 When all the players in a team have taken a kick from the penalty mark, it is not necessary that they follow the same order in taking their second kick as they had for the first series of kicks.

15 If a player who has already been cautioned commits a second cautionable offence at the taking of kicks from the penalty mark, he shall be sent off.

16 If the lights fail at a stadium after extra time but before the taking of kicks from the penalty mark, and if they cannot be repaired in a reasonable time, the referee shall decide the match by tossing a coin or drawing lots.

17 A substitute who has not taken part in the match, including extra time where it is played, may not take part in kicks from the penalty mark, except to replace an injured goalkeeper.

18 After each team has taken 10 kicks from the penalty mark, a team which has had a player sent off may use a player who has already taken a kick for the 11th kick.

19 If at the end of the match some players leave the field of play and fail to return for the taking of kicks from the penalty mark, and are not injured, the Referee will not allow the kicks to be taken and will report the matter to the responsible authorities.

20 If, at the taking of kicks from the penalty mark, or when extended time is being allowed for a penalty-kick to be taken in normal playing time, the ball strikes the goal-post or cross-bar, strikes the goalkeeper and enters the goal, a goal shall be awarded.

The Role of the Fourth Official

1 He would be appointed under the rules of a competition and would officiate in the event of any of the three Match Officials being unable to continue.

2 The organizer, prior to the start of the competition, should state clearly whether, in the event of any Referee being unable to continue, the Fourth Official would take over as the match Referee or whether the senior Assistant Referee would take over as Referee with the Fourth Official becoming an Assistant Referee.

3 The Fourth Official would assist with any administrative duties before, during and after the match as required by the Referee.

4 He would be responsible for assisting with substitution procedures during the match.

5 He would control the replacement footballs where required. If during a match the match ball had to be replaced he would, on the instructions of the Referee, provide another ball thus keeping the time delay to a minimum.

6 He would have the authority to check the equipment of substitutes prior to them entering the field of play. In the event of their equipment not being within the Laws of the Game he would inform the Assistant Referee who would then inform the Referee.

7 The Fourth Official will assist the Referee at all times.

8 After the match the Fourth Official will submit a report to the appropriate authorities, on any misconduct or other incident which has occurred out of the vision of the Referee and the Assistant Referees. The Fourth Official must advise the Referee and his assistants of any report being made.

Signals by the Referee and Assistant Referees

The signals used in this Memorandum have been approved by the International F.A. Board for use by registered Referees of affiliated National Associations. The signals are simple, universally in use and well understood.

1 While it is not the duty of the Referee to explain or mime any offence that has caused him to give a particular decision, there are times when a **simple gesture** or word of guidance can aid communication and assist toward greater understanding, and gaining more respect, to the mutual benefit of both Referee and players. Improving communication should be encouraged, but the **exaggerated miming** of offences can be undignified and confusing and **should not be used**.

2 An indication by the Referee of the point where a throw-in should be taken may well help a player from taking a throw-in improperly. A call of **'Play On: Advantage'** *confirms to the player that the Referee has not missed a foul*, but has chosen to apply advantage. Even an indication that the ball was minutely deflected by touching another player on its path across a touch-line might be helpful in generating a greater understanding between Referee and players. A better understanding will lead to more harmonious relationships.

3 All signals given by the Referee should be simple, clear and instinctive. They should be designed to control the game efficiently and to ensure continuous play as far as is possible; they are intended essentially to indicate what the next action in the game should be, not principally to justify that action.

4 An arm pointing to indicate a corner-kick, goal-kick or foul, and the direction in which the kick is to be taken, will normally be sufficient. **The raised arm to indicate that a free-kick is indirect** is clearly understood, but if a player queries politely whether the award is a direct free-kick or an indirect free-kick, a helpful word from the Referee, in addition to the regular signal, will lead to a better understanding in future.

5 The duties of the Referee and Assistant Referees are set out briefly but clearly in the Laws of the Game, **Laws V** and **VI**.

6 There is a further exposition of co-operation between the Referee and Assistant Referees in the Memorandum explaining the universally adopted system of 'Diagonal Control'.

7 The proper use of the whistle, voice and hand signals by the Referee and the flags by the Assistant Referees should all assist understanding through clear communication.

Co-operation between Assistant Referees and Referee

8 When play has been stopped the Assistant Referee should assist the Referee by signalling in the following manner for the following incidents:

1 **Off-Side.** The Assistant Referee should lower his flag a full arm's length to the positions illustrated, and point across the field of play to indicate the spot from which the kick should be taken. The only exception would be where the Referee has decided to position himself to judge off-side when play develops from a corner-kick, penalty-kick or free-kick close to goal.

2 **Throw-In.** When the ball goes out of play over the touch-line on his side of the field, the Assistant Referee should indicate the direction of the throw. He should also signal if the thrower's feet, at the moment of release of the ball, are incorrectly placed.

3   Corner- and Goal-Kicks. When the whole of the ball goes out of play over the goal-line the Assistant Referee should indicate whether a corner-kick or a goal-kick should be given.

4   Goal. When the Referee indicates that a goal is scored the Assistant Referee should return quickly to his position towards the half-way line.

Law XII. If the Assistant Referee senses that the Referee has not seen an infringement he should raise his flag high. If the Referee stops play the Assistant Referee should indicate the direction of the free-kick (direct or indirect), otherwise he shall lower his flag.

5   Substitution. When a substitution is to be made the Assistant Referee nearest the point of substitution shall attract the attention of the Referee by raising his flag as shown in the illustration included in the colour section.

Memorandum on co-operation between Referees and Assistant Referees

Co-operation between Referee and Assistant Referees – Law VI

In the Laws of the Game set out in the foregoing pages there are no instructions as to the relative positioning of Referee and Assistant Referees during a game. There are, however, instructions in **Laws V and VI** with regard to powers and duties of Referees and Assistant Referees which rightly interpreted would mean co-operation. **Law VI** stipulates that two Assistant Referees shall be appointed, whose duty (subject to the decision of the Referee) shall be:

(a) To indicate WHEN the ball is out of play.
(b) To indicate when the ball has crossed the goal-line and whether a corner-kick or a goal-kick is to be awarded.
(c) To indicate which side is entitled to the throw-in.
(d) To assist the Referee in carrying out the game in accordance with the Laws.

The assistance referred to in (d) is:

(1) Signalling when the WHOLE of the ball is out of play.
(2) Indicating WHICH side is entitled to the corner-kick, the goal-kick, or the throw-in.
(3) Calling the attention of the Referee to rough play or ungentlemanly conduct.
(4) Giving an opinion on any point on which the Referee may consult him.

(5) **Substitution.** When a substitution is to be made, the Assistant Referee nearest to the point of substitution shall attract the attention of the Referee by raising his flag as shown in the illustration included in the colour section.

Neutral Assistant Referees

The assistance referred to above is best given by NEUTRAL ASSISTANT REFEREES. A limitation is placed upon CLUB LINESMEN because points (2), (3) and (4) are not usually referred to those who are not neutral. It is appreciated that there must be a different attitude adopted by the Referee in the case of Assistant Referees, because in effect there are THREE officials supervising the play; the REFEREE remains as principal official, but the Assistant Referees are there to assist him to control the game in a proper manner.

Club Linesmen

To get the most effective co-operation from CLUB LINESMEN the following procedure should be adopted:

(1) BOTH Club Linesmen should report to the Referee BEFORE the start of the match, and receive his instructions, and be informed that no matter what may be their personal opinion the decision of the Referee is final, and must not be questioned.
(2) The work allotted to them as Club Linesmen is to signal WHEN the ball is ENTIRELY over the touch-line, and to indicate WHICH side is entitled to the throw-in, subject always to the decisions of the Referee.

Keeping in mind their distinctive duties outlined above Referees should decide beforehand exactly WHAT they want their Club Linesmen to do, and should be able to tell them distinctly how they can best help him. It is essential that there should be some conference between the three officials BEFORE any match. As the chief of this trio, the Referee must be able to indicate clearly to his assistants how they may best help him. His instructions must be specific, in order to avoid confusion. On their side, the ASSISTANT REFEREES must fully appreciate the Referee's prior authority, and accept his rulings without question, should there be any difference of opinion amongst them. Their relationship to him MUST be one of assistance and neither undue intervention nor opposition.

The Referee will operate the diagonal system of control when his Assistant Referees are neutral. When they are Club Linesmen he shall inform them which method he intends to operate. He will co-operate with his Assistant Referees on the following matters and indicate to them:–

(a) The time by his watch.

(b) The side of the field which each Assistant Referee will take in each half of the match.

(c) Their duties prior to the commencement of the game, such as the examination of the appurtenances of the game.

(d) Which shall be the senior Assistant Referee in case of need.

(e) The position to be taken for corner-kicks.

(f) The sign that he has noticed his Assistant Referee, but has overruled the indication therefrom.

(g) Which action in the throw-in shall be in the province of the Assistant Referee, and which that of the Referee, e.g., many Referees ask their Assistant Referees to watch for foot faults whilst they look for the hand faults.

Referees should not necessarily keep to one diagonal of the field of play. If the state of the ground, wind, sun or other conditions demand a change to the opposite diagonal, a Referee should indicate to his Assistant Referees his intention to make such a change-over, and the Assistant Referees will at once take over the other half of their particular lines. One advantage of such a change of diagonal is that the surface of the ground, next to the touch-line, will be less severely worn because the whole length of the field will be utilized.

Other co-operative matters may be added, but it is important that each of these should be known to the three officials.

The following diagrams illustrate the diagonal system of control, and if studied and practised will lead to uniform methods of control.

The Diagonal System of Control

Diagram One

The imaginary diagonal used by the Referee is the line **A–B**; the cross diagonal used by the Assistant Referee is adjusted to the position of the Referee.

If the Referee is near **A**, Assistant Referee **AR2** will be at a point between **M** and **K**; when the Referee is at **B**, Assistant Referee **AR1** will be between **E** and **F**. This gives TWO Officials control of the respective '*danger zones*', one at each side of the field.

Assistant Referee AR1 adopts the REDS as his side; **Assistant Referee AR2** adopts the BLUES. As RED forwards move towards the BLUE goal, Assistant Referee **AR1** keeps up with their foremost man, so in actual practice he will rarely get into RED's half of the field. Similarly Assistant Referee **AR2** keeps up with the foremost BLUE's player, and will rarely get into BLUE's half.

At **corner-kicks** or **penalty-kicks** the Assistant Referee in that half where the corner-kick or penalty-kick occurs positions himself at **N** and the Referee takes positions illustrated in **Diagram 4**: Corner-kick and **Diagram 9**: Penalty-kick.

The Diagonal System **fails** if Assistant Referee **AR2** gets between **G** and **H** when the Referee is at **B**; or when Assistant Referee **AR1** is near **C** or **D** when the referee is at **A**. Then there are TWO Officials at the same place – **this should be avoided**.

(N.B. – Some Referees prefer to use the opposite diagonal, from F to M, in which case the Assistant Referees should adjust their positions accordingly.)

DIAGRAM 1

DIAGRAM 2

START OF GAME

Position of Referee at Kick-off – R.

Position of Assistant Referees – AR1 and AR2.

Players – ○ and ●.

Diagonal followed by Referee – A —— B.

Referee moves to diagonal along line ←——→ according to direction of attack.

Ball – ⊗.

DIAGRAM 3

DEVELOPMENT OF ATTACK

(From Diagram 2)

Ball moves out to left wing, Referee (R) slightly off diagonal to be near play.
Assistant Referee (AR2) level with spearhead of attack.
Two officials, therefore, up with play.
Assistant Referee (AR1) in position for clearance and possible counter attack.

73

DIAGRAM 4

CORNER-KICK

Position of officials the same no matter at which corner-area the kick is taken. Referee (R) alongside goal-post, or at position shown.

Concerning the position of the Assistant Referee No. 2, in accordance with the instructions from the Referee the Assistant Referee No. 2 (AR2) shall be near the corner flag or on the goal-line near the corner flag, to observe whether the ball is properly played, whether the opposing players are at proper distance (10 yards), whether the ball is behind the goal-line, or whether incidents have happened possibly hidden from the Referee.

Assistant Referee (AR1) in position for clearance and possible counter attack.

DIAGRAM 5

THE COUNTER-ATTACK

(Following Diagram 4)

Referee (R) sprints to regain correct position on diagonal along path ———→
(Note: The Referee who is physically fit is able to do this easily.)
Assistant Referee (AR2) hurries back to his correct position on the touch-line.
Assistant Referee (AR1) level with attack and in position to see infringements
and indicate decisions until Referee regains his position.

DIAGRAM 6

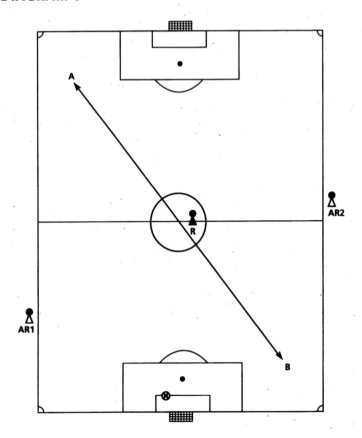

GOAL-KICK

Referee (R) in midfield adjacent to central point of diagonal.
Assistant Referee (AR1) exercising watch over goal-kick.
Assistant Referee (AR2) in position pending a possible attack by side taking goal-kick.

DIAGRAM 7

FREE-KICK IN MIDFIELD

Players lined up for kick ● and ○. Referee (R) and Assistant Referee (AR2) in
respective diagonal positions, level with players and able to judge accurately
any questions of off-side or foul play. Assistant Referee (AR1) sees that kick is
taken from correct position and also is in position for possible counter attack.

77

DIAGRAM 8

FREE-KICK NEAR GOAL

(Just outside penalty-area)

Players ● and ○ line up for free-kick.
Referee (R) takes up his position just off his diagonal so that he is placed accurately to judge off-side. Assistant Referee (AR2) is more advanced but can watch for off-side and fouls and also is in a good position to act as goal judge in the event of a direct shot being taken.

DIAGRAM 9

PENALTY-KICK

Players ● and ○ with the exception of the goalkeeper and kicker are shown outside the penalty area and at least 10 yards from the ball – goalkeeper on goal-line.

Referee (R) is in position to see that kick is properly taken and that no encroachment takes place.

Assistant Referee (AR2) watches goalkeeper to see that he does not advance illegally and also acts as goal judge.

Assistant Referee (AR1) is in position should the goalkeeper save a goal and start a counter attack.

DIAGRAM 10 (A)

THROW-IN

Ball out of play and Assistant Referee (AR2) is in position to indicate position of throw and to which side.

Referee (R) crosses from diagonal to centre of field, in the same manner as a defence covering a throw-in.

Assistant Referee (AR1) watches his forward line against the possible counter attack.

DIAGRAM 10 (B)

THROW-IN

Assistant Referee (AR1) is away from the throw-in but should be able to judge feet and probably to indicate which side is entitled to throw. He also maintains his position in the event of a clearance.

Referee (R) can judge other throw-in infringements and veers slightly from his diagonal towards touch-line.

Assistant Referee (AR2) is in position to see any infringement occurring before Referee can turn to follow play.

Diagrams illustrating points in connection with OFF-SIDE

NOTE: The players marked ⊗ are attacking the goal and those marked ○ are defending.

Direction of movement of the ball — — — — →

Direction of movement of player ————→

DIAGRAM 1 – OFF-SIDE

Pass to a Team Mate

A passes the ball to **B**.

B is off-side because he is in front of **A** and is nearer to his opponents' goal-line than at least two opponents when the ball was passed by **A**.

DIAGRAM 2 – NOT OFF-SIDE

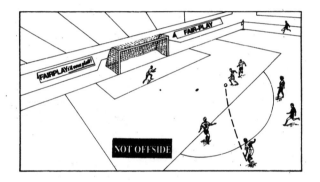

Pass to a Team Mate (continued)

A plays the ball forward to **B** who is level with the second last defender.

B is not off-side since, at the moment the ball was played by **A**, he was not nearer to his opponents' goal-line than at least two of his opponents.

83

DIAGRAM 3 – NOT OFF-SIDE

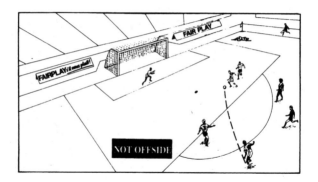

Pass to a Team Mate

A plays the ball forward to **B** who is level with the second last defender.

B is not off-side since, at the moment the ball was played by **A**, he was not nearer to his opponents' goal-line than at least two of his opponents.

Player **C**, lying injured outside the penalty area, is in an off-side position but would not be penalised since he is not involved in active play.

DIAGRAM 4 – NOT OFF-SIDE

Pass to a Team Mate (continued)

A plays the ball to B who is level with the last two opponents.

B is not off-side since at the moment the ball was played by A, he was not nearer his opponents' goal-line than at least two of his opponents.

85

DIAGRAM 5 – OFF-SIDE

Pass to a Team Mate (continued)

A crosses the ball forward from outside the penalty area.

B runs from Position 1 and collects the ball as it lands at Position 2.

B is off-side since, at the moment the ball was played by **A**, he was nearer to his opponents' goal-line than at least two of his opponents and gained an advantage by being in active play.

DIAGRAM 6 – NOT OFF-SIDE

Pass to a Team Mate (continued)

A passes the ball to **B** who runs from Position 1 to Position 2 to play it.

B is not off-side because at the moment the ball was played by **A**, he was not in an off-side position since he was not in front of the ball and was not nearer to his opponents' goal-line than at least two of his opponents.

DIAGRAM 7 – OFF-SIDE

Inter-passing with a Team Mate

A plays the ball to B from Position 1 and runs forward to receive the return pass.

B plays the ball to A who is now in Position 2.

A is off-side since at the moment the ball was played forward to him by B, he was nearer his opponents' goal-line than at least two of his opponents and gained an advantage by being in active play.

DIAGRAM 8 – OFF-SIDE

Interfering with an Opponent

A shoots for goal and the ball enters the net.

B is standing in front of the goalkeeper.

The goal would not be allowed since B, who is in an off-side position, is involved in active play and is interfering with an opponent.

DIAGRAM 9 – NOT OFF-SIDE

Shot at Goal

A shoots for goal and scores.

Although **B** is in an off-side position, he is not involved in active play and the goal would be allowed.

DIAGRAM 10 – OFF-SIDE

Ball Rebounding from Goal Posts or Crossbar

A shoots for goal and the ball rebounds from the post to **B** who kicks the ball into goal.

The goal would be disallowed since **B**, who was in an off-side position when the ball was last played by **A**, was in active play and gained an advantage by being in that position.

91

DIAGRAM 11 – NOT OFF-SIDE

Not Interfering with an Opponent

A shoots for goal and scores.

Although B is lying injured in an off-side position, he is not involved in active play.

The goal would be allowed.

DIAGRAM 12 – OFF-SIDE

Interfering with an Opponent

A shoots for goal and the ball enters the net.

·B, who is lying injured in the goal area and in the path of the ball, would be penalised for off-side. By his presence, however accidental, he is involved in the active play and is interfering with an opponent.

93

DIAGRAM 13 – OFF-SIDE

Shot Rebounds from Goalkeeper

A shoots the ball at goal and the ball rebounds from the goalkeeper to player **B**.

The goal is disallowed since **B**, who was in an off-side position when the ball was last played by **A**, was in active play and gained an advantage by being in that position.

DIAGRAM 14 – OFF-SIDE

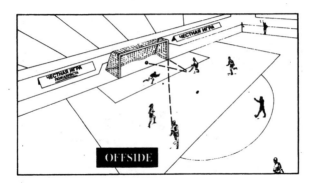

Ball Rebounding from Goal Posts or Crossbar

A shoots for goal and the ball rebounds from the post to **B** who kicks the ball into goal.

The goal is disallowed since **B**, who was in an off-side position when the ball was last played by **A**, was in active play and gained an advantage by being in that position.

95

DIAGRAM 15 – OFF-SIDE

Corner Kick

A takes a corner kick and the ball goes to **B**.

B shoots for goal and the ball is touched by **C** and enters the goal. The goal is not permitted since **C** was in front of the ball and there were not at least two opponents between him and the goal-line when it was last played by **B**.

DIAGRAM 16 – NOT OFF-SIDE

Corner Kick

A corner kick is taken by **A** and the ball goes to **B** who scores.

Although **B** has only one opponent between him and the goal-line, the goal is allowed since a player cannot be off-side if he receives the ball direct from a corner kick.

97

DIAGRAM 17 – NOT OFF-SIDE

Throw-in

A throws the ball to **B** who scores.

The goal is allowed.

Although **B** is in front of the ball and there is only one opponent between him and the goal-line, he is not off-side because a player cannot be offside if he receives the ball direct from a throw-in.

DIAGRAM 18 – NOT OFF-SIDE

Pass to a Team Mate

B plays the ball ahead of A who is in his own half.

Although there are not at least two opponents nearer their own goal-line at the moment when B played the ball, A is not off-side since a player cannot be offside in his own half of the field of play.

DIAGRAM 19(A), (B) – NOT OFF-SIDE

(a) The ball is kicked to the goalkeeper by defender **X**. An attacking player **A** runs towards the goalkeeper to challenge him.

(b) The goalkeeper kicks the ball up-field and the attacking player **A** turns to take up an onside position.

DIAGRAM 19(C) – NOT OFF-SIDE

(c) The ball is intercepted by player **B**, a team mate of the attacking player. It is transferred to another team mate, player **C**, on the wing.

Although the attacking player **A** is in an off-side position, he would not be penalised since he is not involved in active play.

Diagrams illustrating some aspects of SERIOUS FOUL PLAY

1

The attacker, number 9, is making his way towards goal with an obvious goalscoring opportunity when he is (intentionally) tripped by a defender.

According to International FA Board Decision 15, this would be regarded as serious foul play and the defender must be sent off.

2

An attacker is making his way towards goal when he is (intentionally) tripped by an opponent. He did not, however, have an obvious goalscoring opportunity.

According to International FA Board Decision 15, this would not be regarded as serious foul play.

3

FIFA FAIR PLAY

An attacker making his way to goal with an obvious goalscoring opportunity attempts to move past the goalkeeper who (intentionally) holds him. A penalty kick is awarded.

According to International FA Board Decision 15, this would be regarded as serious foul play and the goalkeeper must be sent off.

4

FIFA FAIR PLAY

An attacker is (intentionally) held by the goalkeeper inside the penalty area and a penalty kick is awarded.

The attacker is moving away from goal and so does not have an obvious goalscoring opportunity.

According to International FA Board Decision 15, this would not be regarded as serious foul play.

5

The attacker is (intentionally) tripped inside the penalty area and a penalty kick is awarded. There was, however, no obvious goalscoring opportunity since the player was moving away from goal.

According to International FA Decision 15, this would not be regarded as serious foul play.

6

The attacker, number 11, is (intentionally) tripped but there is no obvious goalscoring opportunity since he is not moving towards goal.

According to International FA Decision 15, this would not be regarded as serious foul play.

7

An attacker shoots for goal but an outfield player punches the ball over the bar, thus preventing a goal being scored.

According to International FA Board Decision 16, this player is guilty of serious foul play and must be sent off.

If the defender had intentionally punched or handled the ball and the ball had entered the goal he would not have been guilty of serious foul play according to International FA Board Decision 16, but he should be cautioned for ungentlemanly conduct.

8

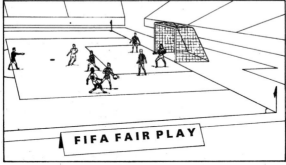

An attacker, number 10, plays the ball and it is intentionally handled by a defender inside the penalty area. A penalty kick would be awarded.

According to International FA Board Decision 16, this would not be regarded as serious foul play.

If the ball had struck the defender on the hand accidentally no offence would have been committed and play would have been allowed to continue.

9

The attacker, number 11, is running on to a forward pass and has an obvious goalscoring opportunity. A defender jumps up and deliberately handles the ball thus preventing an obvious goalscoring opportunity.

According to International FA Board Decision 16, this player is guilty of serious foul play and must be sent off.

10

An attacker is running on to a forward pass with an obvious goalscoring opportunity when the goalkeeper rushes from his goal and intentionally handles the ball outside the penalty area.

According to International FA Board Decision 16, the goalkeeper is guilty of serious foul play and must be sent off.

Videos

Code	Title	Unit	Post	Total
	SOCCER TACTICS & SKILLS VIDEOS			
VID001	Attacking in the Attacking 3rd of the Field	£23.44	£0.70	£24.14
VID002	Passing & Support	£23.44	£0.70	£24.14
VID003	Creating Space	£23.44	£0.70	£24.14
VID004	Defending	£23.44	£0.70	£24.14
VID005	Defending & Attacking Free Kicks & Corners	£23.44	£0.70	£24.14
VID006	Shooting	£23.44	£0.70	£24.14
VID007	Goalkeeping	£23.44	£0.70	£24.14
VID008	Complete Set – Including a free copy of book	£164.08	£8.35	£172.43
	THE WINNING FORMULA VIDEOS			
VID010	Direct Play	£11.99	£0.88	£12.87
VID011	Scoring	£11.99	£0.88	£12.87
VID012	Winning the Advantage	£11.99	£0.88	£12.87
VID013	Defending to Win	£11.99	£0.88	£12.87
VID014	Goalkeeping	£11.99	£0.88	£12.87
VID015	Complete Set	£49.95	£3.80	£53.75
VID020	Soccer Star Video	£10.95	£0.77	£11.72

All these video tapes and all publications are available from:–
FA Publications,
9 Wyllyotts Place,
Potters Bar,
Herts. EN6 2JD.

Payment may be made by credit card (Visa/Access only)
by telephoning 'FA Publications' on **01707 651840**.

Publications
1996/97

Code	Title	Total
	PUBLICATIONS	
PUB006	Soccer Tactics & Skills	£10.99
PUB007	The Winning Formula	£9.99
PUB019	Coaching & Teaching with Disabilities	£2.95
PUB010	Soccer Star Book	£3.00
PUB018	Soccer Star Challenge Pack	£3.00
NVQ001	Football Curriculum Guide	£9.50
PUB001	FA Diary 1996/97 (Available August '96)	£4.99
PUB002	FA Yearbook 1996/97	£6.99
PUB003	FA Handbook 1996/97	£5.00
PUB017	FA News Annual 1995/96	£2.50
PUB011	Laws of Association Football (Ref. Chart)	£4.99
PUB012	Arrangement of Fixtures	£1.00
PUB013	Know The Game Soccer	£3.99
PUB015	Flying Start Soccer (hard cover)	£6.50
PUB016	Flying Start Soccer (soft cover)	£2.95
PUB022	Official History of The FA	£16.95
PUB024	Soccer Referee's Manual	£10.99